Copyright © by Shanillia26

Independently Published
ISBN: 9798704349181

First Printing, 2021

Shanillia26
The Netherlands

www.Shanillia26.com

Copyright

Preface

Dear reader,

This book is dedicated to my daughters Shanillia and Janelle, my biggest Blessings.

I have always been deeply dedicated to raising Shanillia & Janelle into Fierce Black Women.

Women who feel so comfortable in their skin, that it inspires those around them to dare and stand in their power too.

Let this book be a testimony of that.

Thank you for your continuous support.

Love,

Soraja aka Shanillia26

Let's get started!

This book is filled with 111 hairstyles for you and your little one to try!

Most hairstyles have a QR code on the page that links you straight to the hairstyle tutorial on Youtube or Instagram.

The tutorial contains all the information you need to know and mentions all the steps, hair products and accessories needed.

How to scan a QR code:

01. Open the Camera app of your smartphone

02. Select the rear facing camera

03. Hold your phone over the QR Code so that it's

clearly visible within your smartphone's

screen

04. Tap the notification to open the link. It

may take a few seconds on most devices.

Have fun!

User Guide

Contents

Who said Healthy Hair should be Boring?!

01.
POODLEPUFF
HAIRSTYLES

TESTIMONY OF A FOLLOWER

''Poodlepuffs was the first style of yours I
tried on my daughter. It gave me the
confidence to do more, thank you''

STYLE 1

GORGEOUS POODLEPUFF HAIRSTYLE

40 MIN STYLES

2. Flat Poodlepuffs

60 MIN STYLE

3. Duo Poodlepuffs & Braids

45 MIN STYLE

STYLE 4

POODLEPUFF PONYTAIL

40 MIN STYLES

5. Poodlepuff Pigtails

**30
MIN
STYLE**

6. Poodlepuff Ponytail

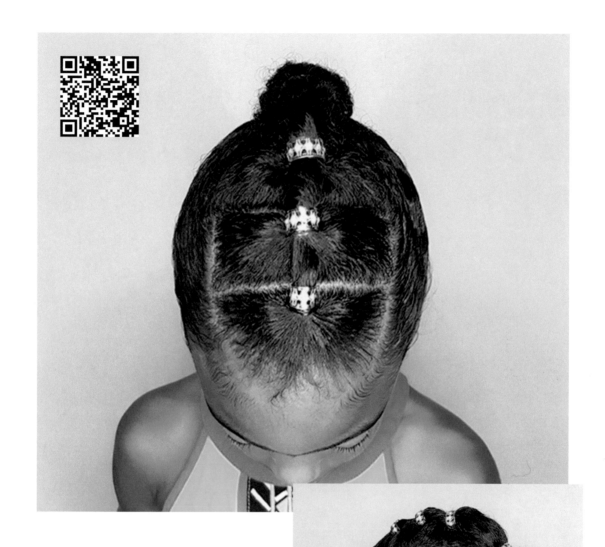

40 MIN STYLE

STYLE 7

BLACK GIRL MAGIC POODLEPUFFS

180 MIN STYLES

8. Jumbo Poodlepuffponytail

30 MIN STYLE

9. Poodlepuff Ponytails

40-60 MIN STYLE

STYLE 10

PERFECT FOR THE HOLIDAYS!

40 MIN STYLES

11. Buns & Poodlepuffs

40 MIN STYLE

12. Purple Poodlepuff Pigtails

40 MIN STYLE

02. BUN HAIRSTYLES

TESTIMONY OF A FOLLOWER

"I love how you do their hair!
it's definitely inspiration even for me"

13. Buns & Braids

30 MIN STYLE

14. Braids & Buns

40 MIN STYLE

STYLE 15

AMAZING BUN HAIRSTYLE!

30 MIN STYLES

STYLE 16

BUNS & BRAIDS

45 MIN STYLE

17. Bun & Flattwists

40 MIN STYLE

18. Amazing bun hairstyle

**30-40
MIN
STYLE**

Buns & Braids- Hairstyles for girls

19. BUNS & BRAIDS

20. Amazing Bun hairstyle

30-40 MIN STYLE

STYLE 21

AMAZING BUN HAIRSTYLE

40 MIN STYLES

22. Fulani Braids & Buns

45 MIN STYLE

23. Braided Bun

60-90 MIN STYLE

STYLE 24

HEART BRAIDS & LOVE BUN

30-40 MIN STYLE

25. Bun & Braids

40-60 MIN STYLE

40 MIN STYLE
Teenage protective hairstyle for girls

26.

27. Braids & Buns

40-60 MIN STYLE

28. Holiday Hairstyle Inspo

30 MIN STYLE

STYLE 29

30. Fulani inspired Bun

30-40 MIN STYLE

31. Pull-through Braided Bun

30 MIN STYLE

TODDLER STYLE

Hairstyle that doesn't take long at all!

32.

30 MIN
STYLE

33. Fulani Bun

30 MIN STYLE

34. Toddler hairstyle

30-40 MIN STYLE

BRAIDS & BUNS

45 MIN STYLE

STYLE 36

AMAZING BUN HAIRSTYLE

40-60 MIN STYLES

37. Mommy & daughter hairstyle

30 MIN STYLE

STYLE 38

60-90 MIN STYLE

39. Skai Jackson Bun

30 MIN STYLE

STYLE 40

BUN & BRAIDS

40-60 MIN STYLES

03. PIGTAIL HAIRSTYLES

TESTIMONY OF A FOLLOWER

''My daughter said to me just now, ''mommy I want my hair to look like hers when I get older.'' My daughter is 4yr old and it feels good that she can see young girls that looks like her, can also grow long beautiful hair. #wearebeautiful #melaninpoppin #queens''

STYLE 41

HAIR LOVE!

45 MIN STYLE

42. Toddler hairstyle

30-40 MIN STYLE

STYLE 43

CUTE BUBBLE FISHTAIL BRAIDS PONYTAILS

40 MIN HAIRSTYLE

STYLE 44

BEADS & HAIRBALLIES

20 MIN STYLES

45. Crossed Braids

30-40 MIN STYLE

STYLE 46

CUTE 3 IN ONE FLATBRAIDS

47. ZigZag Braids & Pigtails

30-40
MIN
STYLE

MODERN PIGTAILS

45 MIN STYLE

NOT YOUR AVERAGE CORNROW

40 MIN STYLE

49.

STYLE 50

TWIST & BRAIDS PONYTAILS

45 MIN STYLE

51. Braids & Pigtails

@shanillia26

30 MIN STYLE

STYLE 52

SWEET BOWS & PONYTAILS

04. PONYTAIL HAIRSTYLES

TESTIMONY OF A FOLLOWER

I have enjoyed watching your daughters grow! So happy to see how much the foundational work matters. Truly.

STYLE 53

FAUX STITCH- & PULL-THROUGH BRAIDS

40-60 MIN STYLES

54. Curly Puff

@shanillia26

@shanillia26

10 MIN STYLE

55. High Puff & Braids

30 MIN STYLE

56. High Puff & Braids

40-60 MIN STYLE

57. Jumbo Ponytail & Braided Buns

40 MIN STYLE

STYLE 58

PONYTAIL TWISTS

40 MIN STYLE

59. Stunning Ponytail

30-40 MIN STYLE

60. Cute Ponytail

30-40 MIN STYLE

STYLE 61

OLDSCHOOL HAIRSTYLE WITH NEW SCHOOL TWISTS

60-90 MIN STYLE

62. Braids & Ponytail

45 MIN
STYLE

63. Stunning Ponytail

60 MIN STYLE

STYLE 64
MINI BRAIDS & TUCK AND ROLL

45 MIN STYLE

65. Puff, Bow & Braids

@shanillia26

30-40 MIN STYLE

STYLE 66

BRAIDLESS HAIRSTYLE

20 MIN STYLE

67. Two Braids - One Puff

30 MIN STYLE

STYLE 68

40 MIN STYLES

05. BANTU KNOT HAIRSTYLES

TESTIMONY OF A FOLLOWER

''My daughter said Shanillia looks like her. This gave me so much joy. Representation matters''

69. Golden Bantu Knots

30-40 MIN STYLE

70. Basic Bantu Knots

30-40 MIN STYLE

71. Toddler hairstyle

**30-40
MIN
STYLE**

STYLE 72

THE BLACK UNICORN

60 MIN STYLE

73. Bantu Knots Mohawk

30-40 MIN STYLE

74. Cute Bantu Knots

30-40
MIN
STYLE

75. Mini Side Bantu Knots

30 MIN STYLE

STYLE 76

FULANI INPIRED BRAIDS & BANTUKNOTS

60-90 MIN STYLE

77. Bantu Mohawk

30 MIN STYLE

78. Fingercoils & Bantuknots

45 MIN STYLE

06. HALF UP/HALF DOWN HAIRSTYLES

TESTIMONY OF A FOLLOWER

''I LOVE YOUR PAGE. So much inspiration and love it's intoxicating.''

79. Brownskin Girl Twistout

60 MIN STYLE

STYLE 80

HALF UP/HALF DOWN WAVY STYLE

40 MIN STYLE

81. Bantu & Braids

60-90 MIN STYLE

STYLE 82

CUTE BOW & BRAIDS HAIRSTYLE

60 MIN STYLE

83. Side Braids

40 MIN STYLE

STYLE 84

BUNS WITH HAIRPAINTWAX

45 MIN STYLE

85. Jumbo Bantuknots

20 MIN STYLE

STYLE 86

BRAIDS BUNS TWISTS

60 MIN STYLE

87. Toddler hairstyle

30 MIN STYLE

STYLE 88

CORNROWS & TWISTS

45 MIN STYLE

89. Fulani Twist-out

60 MIN STYLE

STYLE 90

CUTE BANTUKNOTS AND TWISTS

60 MIN STYLE

07. SMALL BRAIDS HAIRSTYLES

TESTIMONY OF A FOLLOWER

I absolutely love your videos. I foster 3 black girls and didn't know a thing about how to care for their hair. Thanks to videos like yours and others I've learned lots.

BRAIDED MOHAWK

40-90 MIN STYLES

92. Heart Braids

90 MIN STYLE

93. Bantu Crown & Braids

120 MIN STYLE

STYLE 94

HALO BRAID

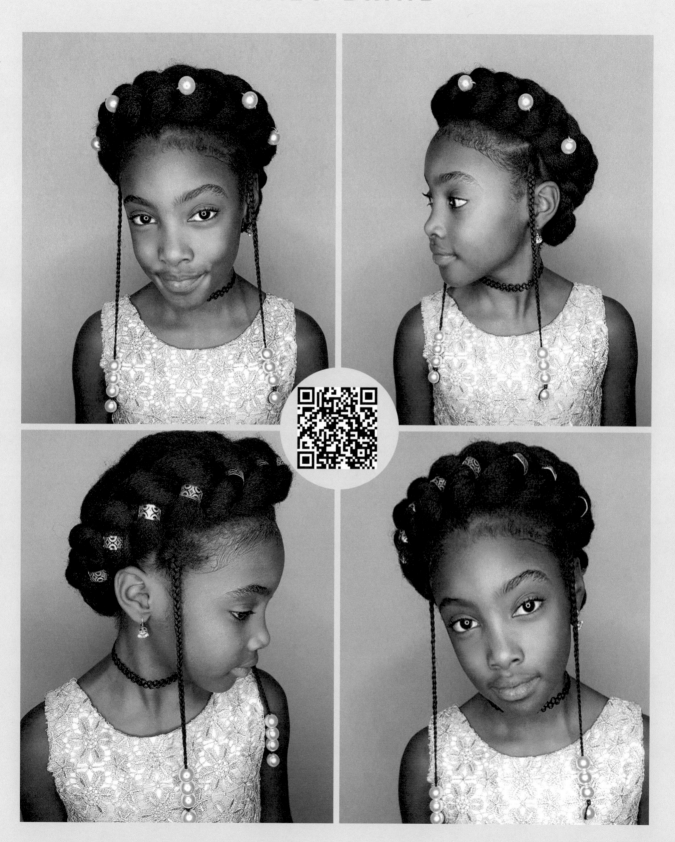

95. Side Braids & Twists

90 MIN STYLE

96. Zig Zag braids & Twists

120 MIN STYLE

STYLE 97

CUTE SIDE BRAIDS

90 MIN STYLE

98. Tuareg hairstyle

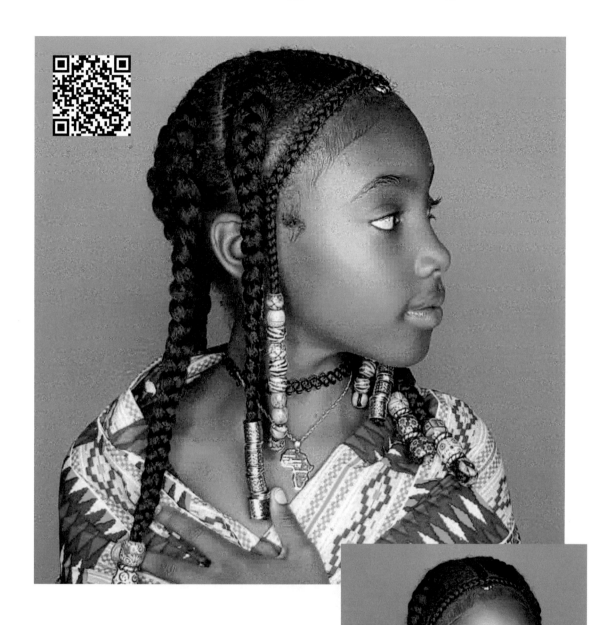

45
MIN
STYLE

99. Box Braids

**90
MIN
STYLE**

STYLE 100

PLAITS BUT FUN!

40-60 MIN STYLES

101. Twisted Frohawk

60 MIN STYLE

102. Knotless Braids

60 MIN STYLE

STYLE 103

MINIBRAIDS MOHAWK

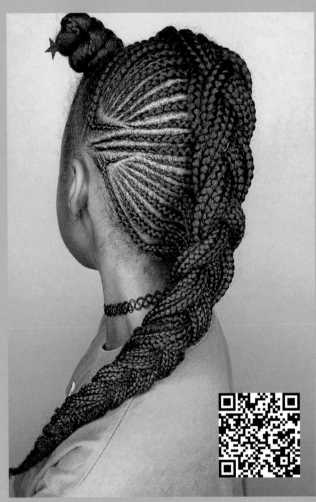

120 MIN STYLE

104. Side Braids & Twists

60 MIN STYLE

105. Mini Twists & Beads

**90
MIN
STYLE**

STYLE 106

FULANI BRAIDS & BEADS

120 MIN STYLE

107. Buns & Mohawk

60-90 MIN STYLE

STYLE 108

SIDE BRAIDS AND PLAITS

60-90 MIN STYLE

109. Cornrows & Twists

90 MIN STYLE

110. Braids & Bantu

90 MIN STYLE

STYLE 111

CORNROWS BUT EXTRA

Thank you for your Support!

● ● ● ● ● ● ● ● ● ● ● ● ● ● ● ● ● ● ● ●

Please follow us on Youtube, Instagram and Facebook for more hairstyle inspiration!

This book is brought to you by:
@shanillia26

Made in the USA
Columbia, SC
14 December 2024

49426984R00069